COUNTRIES

Popcorn

The United Kingdom

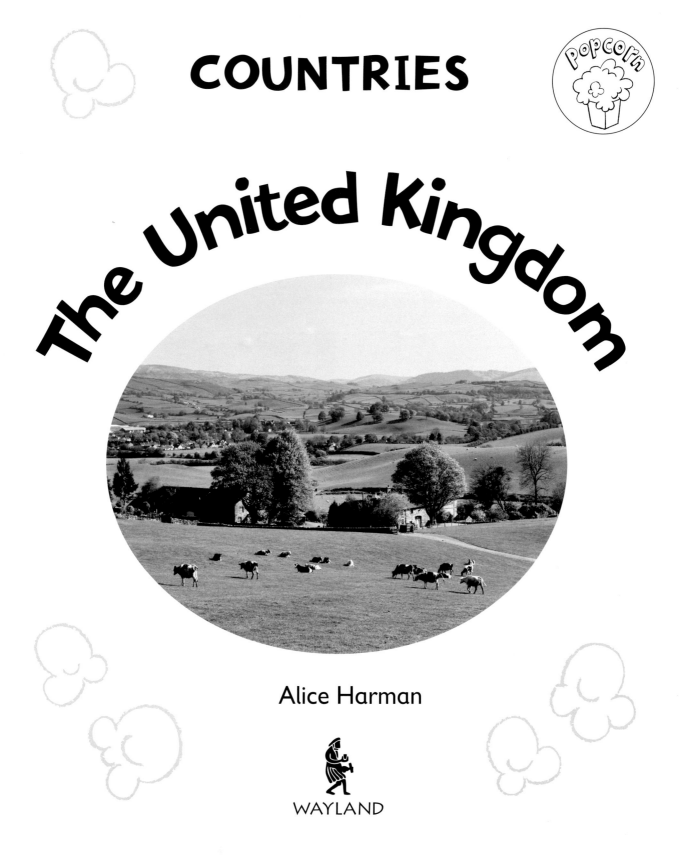

Alice Harman

WAYLAND

Explore the world with **Popcorn** - your complete first non-fiction library.

Look out for more titles in the Popcorn range. All books have the same format of simple text and striking images. Text is carefully matched to the pictures to help readers to identify and understand key vocabulary.
www.waylandbooks.co.uk/popcorn

First published in 2013 by Wayland
Copyright © Wayland 2013

Wayland
Hachette Children's Books
338 Euston Road
London NW1 3BH

Wayland Australia
Level 17/207 Kent Street
Sydney NSW 2000

Produced for Wayland by
White-Thomson Publishing Ltd
www.wtpub.co.uk
+44 (0)843 208 7460

Editor: Alice Harman
Designer: Clare Nicholas
Picture researchers: Alice Harman
Series consultant: Kate Ruttle
Design concept: Paul Cherrill

British Library Cataloging in Publication Data
Harman, Alice.
   UK.
   1. Great Britain--Social conditions--Juvenile literature.
   2. Great Britain--Social life and customs--Juvenile literature.
   3. Great Britain--Geography--Juvenile literature.
   I. Title II. United Kingdom
   941'.08612-dc23

ISBN: 978 0 7502 7086 1

Wayland is a division of Hachette Children's Books,
an Hachette UK company.
www.hachette.co.uk

Printed and bound in China

Picture Credits:
Alamy: Chris Howes/Wild Places Photography 14, Alan Novelli 20; Peter Bull 23; Stefan Chabluk 4; Dreamstime: Piero Cruciatti 19; Andrew Godfrey 21; Shutterstock: timages 5tr, Merlindo 5tl, tazzymoto 5br, Brendan Howard 5bl, John A Cameron 6, Pecold 7, Igor Kozel 8, Christopher Elwell 9, David Milnes 10, Kevin Eaves 11, Dariusz Gora 11 inset, r.nagy 12, Jenny Solomon 15, Jenny Solomon 15 inset, Joe Gough 16t, Jiri Hera 16b, Juriah Mosin 17t, Robert Anthony 17m, Lesley Rigg 17b, Sportsphotographer.eu 18, Christoff 22tr, Nicku 22br, Nicku 22tl, Aleksandar Mijatovic 22bl.

Every effort has been made to clear copyright. Should there be any inadvertent omission, please apply to the publisher for rectification.

# Contents

Where is the United Kingdom?

Here is a map of the United Kingdom (UK).

The UK is in Europe.

There are four countries in the UK. They are Wales, Scotland, England and Northern Ireland.

London is the capital of England.

Edinburgh is the capital of Scotland.

Cardiff is the capital of Wales.

Belfast is the capital of Northern Ireland.

Land and sea

The UK has many different types
of land. There are grassy hills,
forests and marshes. Parts of
the UK have lots of mountains.

Snow covers the top of Ben
Nevis mountain in Scotland.

Ben Nevis
is the highest
mountain in
the UK.

The UK has sea all around it. England, Wales and Scotland are on one island. Northern Ireland is on a different island.

The Giant's Causeway is a famous rocky area on the coast of Northern Ireland.

The weather

The weather in the UK is mild. This means it is not very hot or very cold. There are four seasons. These are spring, summer, autumn and winter.

People visit beaches and swim in the sea in the summer.

The south of the UK is warmer
and drier than the north. It can
rain at any time of the year.
It sometimes snows in winter.

Sometimes it rains so much that
rivers overflow and towns are flooded.

Town and country

Most people in the UK live in towns and cities. Some of the biggest cities are Birmingham, Manchester and Glasgow. London is the third largest city in Europe.

The Houses of Parliament are beside the River Thames in London.

Around 8 million people live in London.

Big Ben

Three quarters of all land in the UK is used for farming. Farmers grow crops such as wheat and potatoes. Cows and sheep live in grass fields.

Farmers use tractors to travel on their land and to harvest crops.

11

Homes

People in towns and cities often live in blocks of flats. Some of these buildings have many floors, and are very tall. Hundreds of people can live in one building.

These blocks of flats in Glasgow have 24 floors!

Many families in the UK live in terraced houses. A terraced house is joined to two other houses. The houses make a row along the street.

These terraced houses in England are around 100 years old.

 Shopping

People come to farmers' markets to buy food that is grown or made on nearby farms. Farmers sell fruit and vegetables, cheese, sausages and other products.

This stall has broccoli, red peppers and cucumbers for sale.

There are more than 550 farmers' markets in the UK.

cucumbers

broccoli

red peppers

Bunch of Beetro

The UK has many shopping centres. People can buy clothes, electronics, furniture and lots of other things in these centres.

Many tourists visit the Bullring shopping centre in Birmingham.

15

Food

Fish and chips is a very popular meal in the UK. The fish is coated in batter, a mixture of flour and water, and fried in oil. The chips are pieces of potato fried in oil.

Fish and chips is sometimes eaten with mushy peas. These are very soft cooked peas.

Different parts of the UK have special types of cakes and biscuits.

The Victoria sponge is a traditional English cake. It has cream and raspberry jam in the middle.

Shortbread is often eaten in Scotland. It is made with lots of butter, and it is very crumbly.

Welsh cakes are made with raisins and currants, and covered with sugar.

✚ Sport

Rugby is a popular sport in the UK.
It was first played 200 years ago at a
school in England. Players can kick the
rugby ball or run with it in their hands.

*The other team has to get the ball
off the player before he scores a try.*

The Olympic and Paralympic Games took place in London in the summer of 2012. People came from all over the world to play sports.

There were 46 different sports at the 2012 Olympic and Paralympic Games.

Athletics events such as the high jump and the 100 metre race were held in the Olympic Stadium.

Holidays and festivals

On 5 November each year, people
in the UK celebrate Bonfire Night.
People watch fireworks, stand around
large outdoor fires and light sparklers.

If you're very careful with sparklers, it can be a lot of fun to make patterns in the air with them!

May Day is celebrated on the first
Monday of May. It is a national holiday.
Some people perform traditional
dances, such as maypole dancing.

Children hold on to long ribbons
and dance around the maypole.

Flags of the UK

The flag of the United Kingdom is often called the Union Jack. Three of the countries in the United Kingdom also have their own flags. These countries are Scotland, Wales and England.

Try to match up each flag with the right part of the UK (or the whole of the UK, for the Union Jack).

1) Wales   2) Scotland   3) United Kingdom   4) England

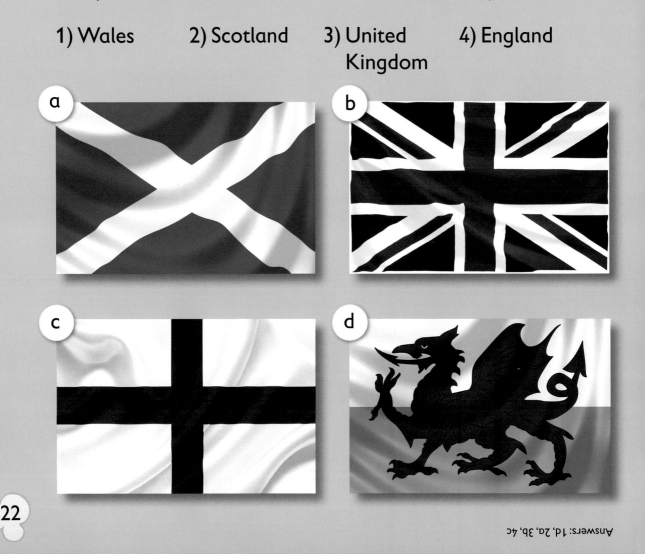

Bake yummy scones

You will need:
- 55g/2oz butter
- 25g/1oz caster sugar
- 1. 225g/8oz self-raising flour
- pinch of salt • 150ml/5fl oz milk
- 1 egg, beaten • large bowl
- pastry brush • pastry cutter

A scone is a small, round, biscuit-like cake. Most people think that scones were first made in Scotland, more than 500 years ago.

1. Ask an adult to turn on the oven to 220C/425F/Gas 7. In a large bowl, use your fingers to rub the butter into the flour and salt. Add the sugar and milk and make a ball of soft dough.

2. Place the dough on a flat surface. Use your hands to flatten it into a round shape that is 2cm (3/4 inch) thick. Cut out smaller circles with the cutter. Put them on a baking tray and brush their tops with beaten egg.

3. Ask an adult to put the scones in the oven. Bake for 12–15 minutes. Leave them to cool, and then spread with butter and jam. Yum!

23

Glossary

capital the city where the government of the country meets

crops plants grown on a farm

crumbly when something easily falls apart into small pieces

currants small dried fruits similar to raisins

flooded covered with water

harvest when a farmer's crops are fully grown, and are gathered to be eaten or sold

marsh grassy land that is often flooded with water

national holiday a day when most people in a country do not have to work or go to school

traditional something that has been part of a culture for a long time

try players score a try in rugby by touching the ball on the ground in a certain area

wheat a plant, part of which is used to make flour

Index

EXPLORE THE WORLD WITH THE POPCORN NON-FICTION LIBRARY!

- Develops children's knowledge and understanding of the world by covering a wide range of topics in a fun, colourful and engaging way
- Simple sentence structure builds readers' confidence
- Text checked by an experienced literacy consultant and primary deputy-head teacher
- Closely matched pictures and text enable children to decode words
- Includes a cross-curricular activity in the back of each book

FREE DOWNLOADS!

OVER 50 TITLES TO CHOOSE FROM!

- Written by an experienced teacher
- Learning objectives clearly marked
- Provides information on where the books fit into the curriculum
- Photocopiable so pupils can take them home

www.waylandbooks.co.uk/downloads